The CAROUSEL Ride

By Lynea Bowdish

Illustrated by Patrick Girouard

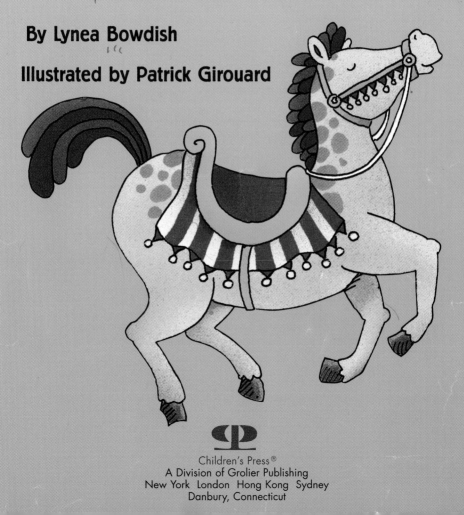

Children's Press®
A Division of Grolier Publishing
New York London Hong Kong Sydney
Danbury, Connecticut

JP
Bowdish

For Bear, Princess, and Chipper, the three best dogs ever!
—L.B.

For John Connolly, who taught me a little art and a lot of confidence.
—P.G.

Reading Consultant
Linda Cornwell
Learning Resource Consultant
Indiana Department of Education

Visit Children's Press® on the Internet at:
http://publishing.grolier.com

Library of Congress Cataloging-in-Publication Data
Bowdish, Lynea.
The carousel ride / by Lynea Bowdish; illustrated by Patrick Girouard.
p. cm. — (Rookie reader)
Summary: On a carousel, Mara imagines herself a queen, a circus star, and the leader of a parade.
ISBN 0-516-20967-1 (lib.bdg.)   0-516-26410-9 (pbk.)
[1. Merry-go-round—Fiction. 2. Imagination—Fiction.] I. Girouard, Patrick, ill. II. Title. III. Series.
PZ7.B67194Car 1998
[E]—dc21

97-43649
CIP
AC

© 1998 Children's Press®, a Division of Grolier Publishing Co., Inc.
Illustration © 1998 by Patrick Girouard

"I'm going on the carousel,"
Mara said.

"Carousels don't go anywhere,"
said her brother.

4

But Mara knew better.

The carousel began.
Up, down, round and round.

Then faster.

Mara was a queen.
She rode through the countryside.
Her people waved.

Up, down, round and round.

Mara was a circus star.
She danced on top of her horse.
The audience clapped.

Up, down, round and round.

Mara was the leader of the parade.
The bands played.
The people cheered.

Up, down, round and round.

The carousel stopped.

"Where have you been?"
Mara's brother said.

27

"Up, down, round and round,"
Mara laughed.

About the Author

Lynea Bowdish's favorite ride has always been the carousel. She loves the splendor of the horses and excitement of the music. Lynea grew up in Brooklyn, New York. She now lives in Hollywood, Maryland, with her husband, David Roberts, their two dogs, a goldfish, and the various animals that show up in the backyard. Lynea taught English on the college level for a number of years. She now spends her time writing and reading children's books.

About the Illustrator

Patrick Girouard always washes his dishes but seldom dries them. He likes to sleep with his head at the foot of the bed. One time he was struck by lightning and was magnetized for seven days. He enjoys drawing pictures, collecting robots, playing with his sons Marc and Max, and going to the show. He lives in Indiana across the street from his sweetheart Rita.